Number Fun

Making Numbers With Your Body

Isabel Thomas

Heinemann
LIBRARY

Chicago, Illinois

Are you ready for some number fun?

Do these things as you look through the book.

- Name the numbers that you see. Find them on the number line.

- Count the number of everyday objects in each picture.

- Find numbers made from straight lines and numbers made from curvy lines.

- Which numbers have straight lines and curvy lines?

- Trace the number shapes with your finger.

- Count the number of children in each picture.

- Name the parts of the body and the colors that you see. The list in the Picture Glossary will help you.

Can you make numbers with your body?

1 2 3 4 5 6 7 8 9 10 11 12 13 14 15 16 17 18 19 20

2

1 2 3 4 5 6 7 8 9 10 11 12 13 14 15 16 17 18 19 20

3

1 2 3 4 5 6 7 8 9 10 11 12 13 14 15 16 17 18 19 20

4

1 2 3 **4** 5 6 7 8 9 10 11 12 13 14 15 16 17 18 19 20

5

1 2 3 4 **5** 6 7 8 9 10 11 12 13 14 15 16 17 18 19 20

6

1 2 3 4 5 6 7 8 9 10 11 12 13 14 15 16 17 18 19 20

7

1 2 3 4 5 6 7 8 9 10 11 12 13 14 15 16 17 18 19 20

8

1 2 3 4 5 6 7 8 9 10 11 12 13 14 15 16 17 18 19 20

9

1 2 3 4 5 6 7 8 9 10 11 12 13 14 15 16 17 18 19 20

10

1 2 3 4 5 6 7 8 9 10 11 12 13 14 15 16 17 18 19 20

1 2 3 4 5 6 7 8 9 10 11 12 13 14 15 16 17 18 19 20

12

⊞ ⊞ ⊞ ⊞ ⊞ ⊞
⊞ ⊞ ⊞ ⊞ ⊞ ⊞

1 2 3 4 5 6 7 8 9 10 11 **12** 13 14 15 16 17 18 19 20

13

1 2 3 4 5 6 7 8 9 10 11 12 13 14 15 16 17 18 19 20

14

● ● ● ● ● ● ●
● ● ● ● ● ● ●

1 2 3 4 5 6 7 8 9 10 11 12 13 14 15 16 17 18 19 20

15

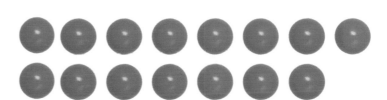

1 2 3 4 5 6 7 8 9 10 11 12 13 14 **15** 16 17 18 19 20

16

1 2 3 4 5 6 7 8 9 10 11 12 13 14 15 **16** 17 18 19 20

17

🌼 🌼 🌼 🌼 🌼 🌼 🌼 🌼 🌼
🌼 🌼 🌼 🌼 🌼 🌼 🌼 🌼

1 2 3 4 5 6 7 8 9 10 11 12 13 14 15 16 17 18 19 20

18

● ● ● ● ● ● ● ● ●
● ● ● ● ● ● ● ● ●

1 2 3 4 5 6 7 8 9 10 11 12 13 14 15 16 17 18 19 20

19

1 2 3 4 5 6 7 8 9 10 11 12 13 14 15 16 17 18 **19** 20

20

1 2 3 4 5 6 7 8 9 10 11 12 13 14 15 16 17 18 19 **20**

My Body: Picture Glossary

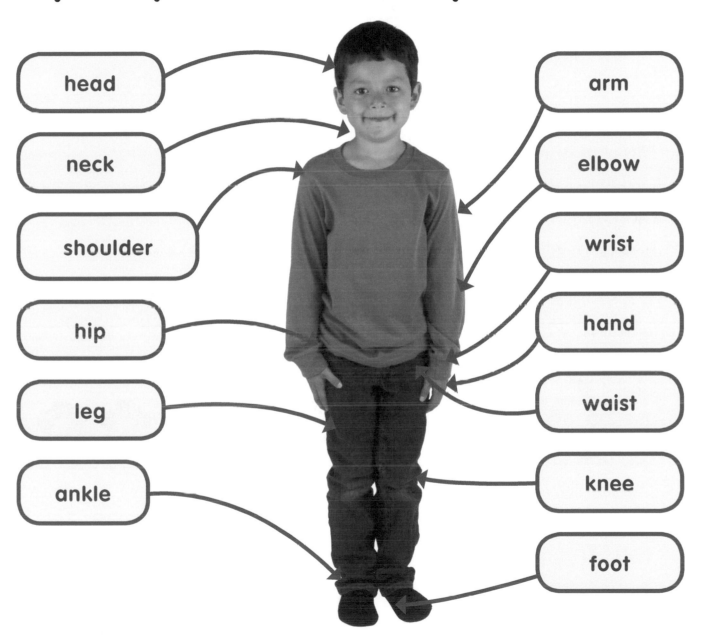

head

neck

shoulder

hip

leg

ankle

arm

elbow

wrist

hand

waist

knee

foot

Number Games

- **Number charades**. One pair or team forms a number with their bodies. The other teams have to guess the number which has been formed.

- **Musical numbers**. Play some music. When the music stops, players use their bodies to form the number called out. Make the game more difficult by asking players to form the number that comes before or after the number called out.

- **Count the steps**. Sit in a large circle. Challenge players one by one to walk, hop, or jump over to another player in a certain number of steps, counting aloud as they move. They can take that player's seat if they make the journey in the right number of steps. If they use too many or too few steps, they have to play again.

- **Tap and count**. Stand in a circle. One player starts by tapping a balloon toward another player and counting aloud: "one." The next player taps the balloon toward another player and counts aloud: "two." If someone drops the balloon, he or she is out and the counting restarts at "one." Continue until there are just two players left. Can the children tap and count all the way up to 100?